W9-AWO-782

The GALAXY GUIDES

WHY DO WE HAVE NIGHT AND DAY?

Alix Wood

PowerKiDS
press

Published in 2016 by **Rosen Publishing**
29 East 21ˢᵗ Street, New York, NY 10010

Editor: Eloise Macgregor
Designer: Alix Wood
Consultant: Kevin E. Yates, Fellow of the Royal Astronomical Society

Photo Credits: Cover, 1, 16, 24 © Shutterstock; 4, 5, 6-7, 8, 22 © Dollar Photo Club; 7 inset, 10, 11, 12, 13, 17, 18, 20, 21, 23 © NASA; 12 © Gregory H. Revera; 14 © Alana Sise; 19 © European Southern Observatory; 23 © Eduemoni; 26 © Jonathan Zdziarski; 27 © iStock

Cataloging-in-Publication Data

Wood, Alix.
Why do we have night and day? / by Alix Wood.
p. cm. — (The galaxy guides)
Includes index.
ISBN 978-1-4994-0850-8 (pbk.)
ISBN 978-1-4994-0849-2 (6 pack)
ISBN 978-1-4994-0848-5 (library binding)
1. Day — Juvenile literature. 2. Night — Juvenile literature.
3. Earth (Planet) — Rotation — Juvenile literature.
4. Sun — Juvenile literature. 5. Moon — Juvenile literature.
I. Wood, Alix. II. Title.
QB633.W66 2016
525'.35—d23

Manufactured in the United States of America

CPSIA Compliance Information: Batch #: WS15PK
For Further Information contact Rosen Publishing, New York, New York at 1-800-237-9932

Contents

Where Does the Daylight Come From? 4

What Is the Sun?.................................6

Where Does the Sun Go at Night? 8

Does the Sun Ever Go Dark? 10

What Is the Moon?................................12

Why Is the Moon Out in the Daytime? 14

Where Do the Stars Go in the Daytime?.........16

Could the Sun Ever Stop Shining? 18

Do Other Planets Have Suns and Moons? 20

Do Other Planets Have Nights and Days? 22

Why Are Some Days Longer Than Others? 24

Could We Live Without the Sun?.....................26

Galaxy Quiz.................................28

Glossary 30

Further Information..................................31

Index and Answers.................................32

Where Does the Daylight Come From?

Have you ever wondered why Earth has nights and days? When you look up at the sky at night it is very different from the sky during the day. The main difference is that it is dark. Why?

The sky is dark because the Sun is no longer visible. We can see the Moon and the stars on a clear night. They light up the dark a little. The Sun is a star too. It is much closer to Earth than other stars. Because it is closer it lights up our sky.

"Sol" is the Latin name for the Sun. We get the name **solar system** from the word. The Sun is not just important because it gives us light. The Sun is the center of our solar system.

What Is the Solar System?

Our solar system has the Sun at its center. Planets, moons, comets, and asteroids all move around the Sun. Objects in space attract other objects to them. This attraction is called **gravity**. Objects with the most **mass** have the strongest pull. Objects such as Earth are pulled toward the Sun because the Sun has a large mass. Meanwhile, other forces try to pull objects away from the Sun. The forces balance each other out, so Earth forever circles the Sun.

the Sun

the solar system

The journey around an object in space is called an **orbit**. How does an orbit happen? Imagine a large cannon on top of an imaginary giant mountain. If the cannon fires a cannonball using low power (A), the ball will curve down and hit Earth. Increase the power (B) and the ball will go further but still hit Earth. If you fire the ball with just the right force (C), as Earth is round, the ground curves away from the ball, so the ball follows a path around Earth. Earth's gravity keeps the ball from going into space.

A
B
C

The Sun is a star. It looks much larger and brighter than other stars because it is closer to Earth. The Sun is very large. It is over 1 million times bigger than Earth!

The Sun is a ball of burning gases. It is mainly made of a gas called **hydrogen**. In the center, the temperature is around 27 million degrees Fahrenheit (15 million degrees Celsius)! Even the temperature at its surface is more than 20 times hotter than a household oven at its highest setting.

HANDS-ON SCIENCE

Make a Simple Pinhole Camera

Never look directly at the Sun as it can damage your eyes. Make this pinhole camera to view the Sun safely.

You will need: 2 sheets of stiff white paper, a pin, a sunny day

Using the pin, punch a hole in the center of one piece of paper. Place your second piece of paper on the ground. Stand with the sun behind you and hold the paper with the hole up. Move it until you see the Sun shine through the hole. Move the paper on the floor so that the Sun image lands on it. What you are seeing is not just a dot of light coming through the hole, but an actual image of the Sun!

The Sun's Layers

The core in the center of the Sun produces the Sun's energy. The layers around the center carry energy outward. The outer layer is called the **photosphere**. Around the outside is the **corona**, which means "crown" in Latin. The corona is faint, so you can't usually see it. Energy from the core typically takes 150,000 years to reach the photosphere, so the light you see today was produced in the Stone Age! It takes another eight and a half minutes for the light from the photosphere to reach Earth.

Where Does the Sun Go at Night?

The Sun doesn't go anywhere, it is always in the same place. Even though you don't feel it, the Earth is spinning all the time. Earth takes 24 hours to completely spin around on its **axis.** When the part of Earth we live on turns away from the Sun we have nighttime. For people on the other side of the Earth it is daytime.

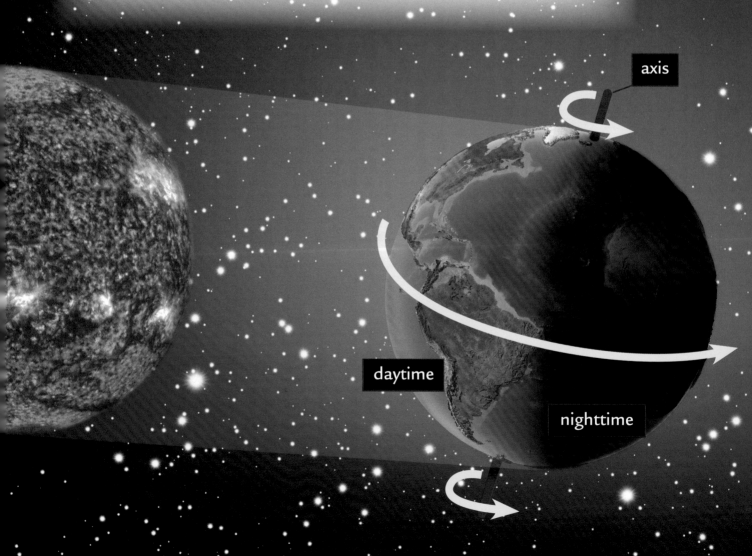

axis

daytime

nighttime

Why Does the Sun Rise in the East and Set in the West?

When viewed from the North Pole the Earth spins **counterclockwise**. As Earth turns toward the Sun and begins to enter its light, it appears as if the sun rises in the east. In fact the Sun stays still and we spin around to face it. As Earth begins to turn away from the Sun's light, the Sun appears to set in the west.

West   East

What it looks like the Sun is doing

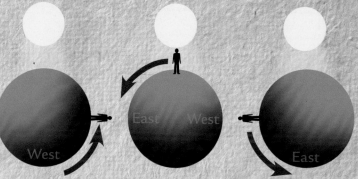

What is actually happening

HANDS-ON SCIENCE

Make a Simple Model Sun and Earth

You will need: a ball, a flashlight, and a small sticker

Place the sticker on the ball. The sticker represents where you live on Earth. Turn the flashlight on, place it about seven paces away, shining on the ball. Now, slowly spin the ball so your sticker is lit up by the flashlight. This is you on Earth during the day. Keep spinning the ball until the sticker is not being lit up by the flashlight. This is you on Earth at night. The flashlight hasn't moved, you have spun so you can no longer see the light.

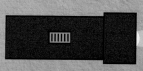

Does the Sun Ever Go Dark?

The Sun doesn't actually go dark, but sometimes the Moon can get in the way of the Sun and block its light. This is called an **eclipse**.

During a solar eclipse the light from the Sun is hidden by the Moon as it passes between Earth and the Sun. Ancient peoples were often afraid of solar eclipses. It must have been terrifying to see the sunlight suddenly disappear without understanding why it was happening.

FACT FILE

Total Solar Eclipse

During a total solar eclipse the Moon completely covers the Sun. The Sun looks like a hole in the sky, with the glow from the corona around the outside of the black circle. Total solar eclipses happen around once every one and a half years. The eclipse lasts around seven and a half minutes, and it takes around an hour before the Sun's full brightness is restored.

A total solar eclipse. The glow around the edge is the corona.

Annular eclipses (pictured right) are when the Moon appears smaller than the Sun as it passes in front. A bright ring of sunlight remains visible during the eclipse. The Moon appears smaller because it is at a point in its orbit when it is farthest away from Earth.

HANDS-ON SCIENCE

Make a Solar Eclipse!

You will need: a flashlight, an orange, some clay, a ruler

Make a ball of clay around a quarter the size of the orange. Place the orange and the clay ball in a line on a table, about 8 inches (20 cm) apart. Stand about 2 feet (60 cm) away from the table with the flashlight at the same level as the clay and the orange. Shine the flashlight at the clay ball so it casts a shadow on the orange. The clay represents the Moon, the flashlight is the Sun, and the orange is the Earth. When the Moon blocks the Sun it casts a shadow on Earth.

Sun   Moon   Earth

What Is the Moon?

The Moon is believed to have been made 4.5 billion years ago when a large object hit the Earth. Rocks which were blasted outward after the impact began to orbit Earth, then joined together to become the Moon.

You can look at the surface of the Moon using a pair of binoculars or a small telescope. The Moon's surface shows the damage caused by rocks of all sizes hitting it over billions of years. The surface is covered in craters, pits, and scars. From Earth we only see one side of the Moon. The other side is always turned away from us.

crater

Why Does the Moon Change Shape?

FACT FILE

We only see the Moon in the night sky because it is lit up by the Sun. It has no light source itself, as it is made of rock. As the Moon moves around Earth we can see it lit up by the Sun from different angles. Being lit from different angles is what produces the changing shapes. These shapes are known as the **lunar phases.** The Moon takes one month to travel all the way around Earth. In that time it changes from a thin crescent to a full moon and back again to a crescent.

The phases of the Moon. The inner circle shows how the Sun lights the Moon during its orbit. The outer circle shows what the Moon looks like to us on Earth during that phase.

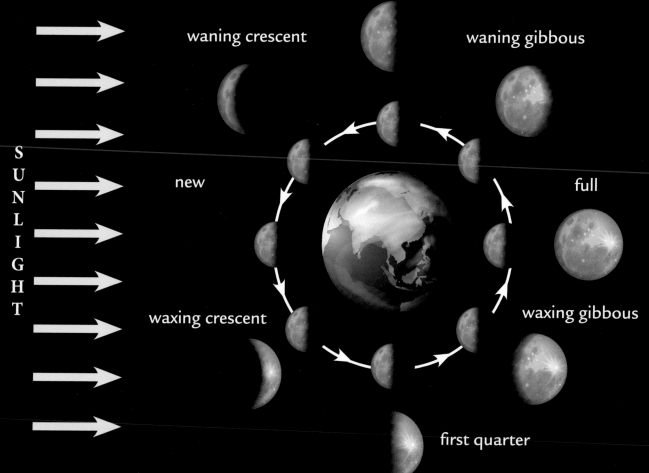

Why Is the Moon Out in the Daytime?

The Moon rises and sets every day, like the Sun. The Sun always rises in the morning and sets in the evening. The Moon rises and sets at a different time every day.

On the day of a new moon, the Moon rises when the Sun rises, crosses the sky at the same time, and sets when the Sun sets. We can't see the new moon as it is too close to the Sun's glare and its lit side is facing away from us.

As the Moon orbits Earth it starts to lag more and more behind the Sun, by around 50 minutes a day. A few days after a new moon we start to see it in the sky after sunset. By first quarter, the Moon is six hours behind the Sun. It rises in the middle of the day and sets in the middle of the night. At full moon, the Moon is opposite the Sun and 12 hours behind it, so it rises as the Sun is setting and sets at sunrise. By last quarter, the Moon lags 18 hours behind the Sun, rising in the middle of the night and setting in the middle of the day.

The Moon appears to glow in the sky because its surface reflects light from the Sun. Its brightness changes depending on where it is in its orbit. A full moon is brightest. Just before and after a new moon we only see a thin sliver of Moon. We can often just make out the rest of the Moon too. This is a result of something called **earthshine**, where the Moon's dark area is slightly lit by sunlight reflecting from Earth's surface.

HANDS-ON SCIENCE

How Does The Moon Glow?

You will need: 2 pieces of white paper, a cardboard box, a flashlight, a few books, some tape

Place the cardboard box 1 foot (30 cm) away from a wall. Tape a piece of white paper onto the box. Tape the second piece of white paper onto the wall in front of the cardboard box. Stack some books beside the paper on the wall. Place the flashlight on the books and point the light at the paper on the box. Adjust the height so the flashlight points at the middle of the paper. Turn off any overhead lights. You should be able to see a circle of light on the paper on the wall even though you're shining the flashlight in the opposite direction.

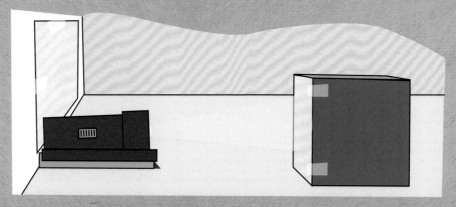

Stars shine very brightly at night. Have you ever wondered why you can't see them in the daytime? The stars don't disappear. They are always in the sky, you just can't see them.

There is one star that you can always see in the sky in the daytime. The Sun is Earth's closest star. We can't see the other stars because the Sun is so bright. It is hard to pick out the weaker stars against the light. When the Sun's light starts to fade at the end of the day, you can see the stars.

HANDS-ON SCIENCE

Light Pollution

Why can you see more stars in the countryside? Light pollution is a problem in many cities. Streetlights and neon signs create a glow in the night sky so it's hard to see the stars. Try this test to see if your area suffers from light pollution. On a clear night switch off any house lights that shine outside. Let your eyes adjust, and look at all the stars. Now ask someone to turn on an outside light. Are the stars as clear as they were?

Which other stars can you see in the daytime?

One of the brightest stars in the sky is called Sirius. You can sometimes see it at sunrise and sunset. Sirius is about eight **light-years** away from Earth. Distance in space is measured in light-years. A light-year is the distance traveled by a beam of light in one year. It is a useful way of measuring the huge distances in space. The light you are seeing from Sirius left the star eight years before you see it and traveled through space for all that time!

Sirius is about twice as large and 25 times brighter than the Sun.

These three bright stars in a line are called "Orion's belt."

FACT FILE

What makes a star shine?

Stars are hot balls of glowing gases and dust held together by their own gravity. The pressure of the layers of gases pressing down towards the core makes their center heat up by a process called **nuclear fusion**. Stars give off light because they are hot. Cool stars glow red. Really hot stars glow white or blue-white.

Could the Sun Ever Stop Shining?

The Sun will one day stop shining, but not for a very, very long time. Stars shine because of the energy in their cores. The energy is produced by hydrogen gas. In around 5 billion years, the hydrogen in the Sun's core will run out and it will not have enough fuel. Then the Sun will stop shining.

We know that the Sun has used up about half of its hydrogen fuel in the last 4.6 billion years, since its birth. It still has enough hydrogen to last between five and seven billion years.

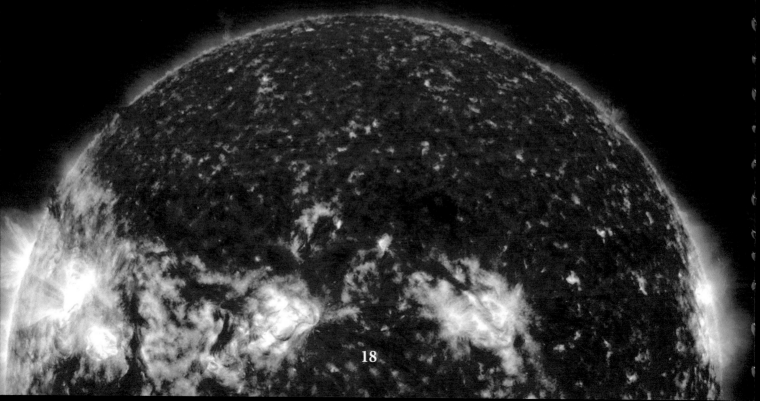

What Will Happen to the Sun?

From studying other stars, scientists can predict what will happen to the Sun. Gradually the Sun will start to burn brighter. In around 1 billion years it will be 10 percent brighter than it is now. In 3.5 billion years it will be 40 percent brighter. It will be so hot that our oceans will boil, and no life could survive on Earth. After around 6 billion years the Sun will run out of hydrogen. The core will heat up and the Sun will get larger, becoming what is known as a **red giant**. After another 100 million years the red giant will blast off its outer layer into a giant ring known as a **planetary nebula** and become a **white dwarf**, slowly cooling down over a trillion years.

red giant phase

the Sun gradually getting larger

planetary nebula

Do Other Planets Have Suns and Moons?

Many other planets in our galaxy have their own moons. There are 146 known moons in our solar system. Earth only has one moon, and Mars only has two. Some other planets have many more. Mercury and Venus have no moons.

Some of the moons in our solar system

Triton

Tethys

Dione

Titan

Iapetus

Mimas

Earth's Moon

Rhea

Enceladus

Europa

Titania

Miranda

Callisto

Oberon

Ganymede

Io

Charon

What Planet Has the Most Moons?

The planets that are closest to the Sun have fewer moons than the ones that are farther away. Outer planets are more massive and therefore have stronger gravitational fields which can sweep up passing objects. Jupiter has the most moons, with at least 67! Four of Jupiter's moons were discovered in 1610 by Galileo Galilei. They were the first objects found to orbit a body that was neither Earth nor the Sun. The most massive moon is Ganymede. It is the ninth largest object in the solar system, larger than the planet Mercury.

Jupiter

There are many stars that have planets orbiting around them, and we are discovering new planets and suns all the time. Stars are giant balls of hot gas, just like our Sun. How long a star lasts depends on how big it is. The biggest stars are hottest and use up their fuel quicker. Small stars may live for trillions of years.

Our Sun is an average to small-size star, known as a **dwarf star**. The largest known star, UY Scuti, is 1,708 times the diameter of the Sun. Stars like these are called giant or supergiant stars. Stars can be different colors depending on how hot they are. Cool stars look red, hot stars look blue-white.

Do Other Planets Have Nights and Days?

The planets in our solar system spin as they move around the Sun. As they spin they experience nights and days just as we do. One complete spin is measured as a day. Some planets spin faster than Earth and some are much slower. This means there are differences in the length of their days.

Mercury has very long days. Mercury takes 58 days and 15 hours to spin around. A day on Mercury is only a little shorter than its year! A year is how long a planet takes to orbit the Sun.

Venus is the slowest moving planet and has the longest day. A day on Venus is 243 Earth days. A day on Venus is actually longer than its year! It only takes 224.7 Earth days to orbit the Sun.

planets in our solar system

Neptune

Venus

Mars

Jupiter

Saturn

Uranus

Mercury

Earth

A day on Mars is very similar to a day on Earth. Mars takes 24 hours 39 minutes and 35 seconds to rotate.

Jupiter is the largest planet, and it has the shortest day. It takes 9.9 hours to complete a rotation.

A day on Saturn was measured at 10 hours 39 minutes in the 1980s. In 2006, astronomers with more advanced equipment got a measurement of about 10 hours and 47 minutes.

A day on Uranus only takes 17 hours 14 minutes.

A day on Neptune lasts 16 hours 6 minutes.

FACT FILE

What About Pluto?

Pluto used to be classified as a planet, but now it is classified as a **dwarf planet**. As planets form, they become the dominant body in their orbit. When they meet other objects they either consume them or force them away with their gravity. Pluto is not that dominant in its orbit, which makes it a dwarf planet. Pluto is also so far from the Sun that the Sun would look more like a very bright star in its sky. The light Pluto receives from the Sun would not be strong enough to create daylight as we know it.

Pluto

Why Are Some Days Longer Than Others?

Have you ever noticed that the days are shorter in winter, and longer in summer? In summer, the northern hemisphere is tilted towards the Sun, so the Sun climbs higher in the sky and therefore spends longer in the sky from sunrise to sunset.

The Earth's Tilt

If you drew an imaginary line around the center of Earth, known as the **equator**, the area above that line is the northern hemisphere. The area below the line is the southern hemisphere. When the North Pole tilts toward the sun it is summer in the northern hemisphere and winter in the southern hemisphere. When it tilts away from the sun it is winter in the northern hemisphere and summer in the southern hemisphere. The angle makes the Sun's rays weaker in the half of the Earth tilted away.

axis — North Pole

northern hemisphere

summer

winter

southern hemisphere

winter

summer

HANDS-ON SCIENCE

The Angle of the Sun and the Seasons

See if you can prove that angled sunlight is cooler than direct sunlight. Try this experiment.

You will need: sheet of graph paper, flashlight, ruler, tape

1. Place the graph paper on a flat surface. Tape the ruler securely to the flashlight so that most of the ruler is sticking out toward where the beam will shine. Hold the flashlight so that the beam shines directly down onto the graph paper. Record how many squares are lit by the beam of light.

2. Then hold the flashlight at a 45-degree angle to the graph paper, using the ruler to make sure it is still the same distance away. Record how many squares are now lit by the flashlight beam. Which angle produced the most lit-up squares? When the beam of light is spread over more squares, that same energy is shared over a larger area, so the heat on each square is less.

45 degrees

Summer is warmer than winter because the Sun's rays hit the Earth at a more direct angle during summer. Also the days are much longer than the nights during the summer so the Earth and the oceans have less time to cool down overnight. During the winter, the Sun's rays hit Earth at an extreme angle. The days are very short, too.

Could We Live Without the Sun?

The Sun gives us light, heat, and energy. Without it, Earth would be cold, and no living thing would be able to survive. The Sun is vital for Earth's survival in many ways.

The Sun's gravity holds the planets in their orbits. If the Sun didn't exist, the planets would float off into the Universe. People need sunlight to help our bodies produce certain vitamins. Plants use the Sun's energy to make them grow. People and animals either eat plants, or eat other animals who eat plants. Even if some animals could survive the extreme cold, they would die because their food source had died.

Any energy we might use to replace the heat of the Sun would run out, too. Solar energy comes directly from the Sun. Oil and coal is made from dead plants and animals. Even wind energy comes from the Sun's heat causing air to move.

How Long Would People Survive Without the Sun?

FACT FILE

The Earth would become dark and start to cool eight and a half minutes after the Sun disappeared, because the light takes that long to reach us. After a week, the warmest places on Earth would be around 0 degrees Fahrenheit (-18 degrees Celsius). After a few months the temperature would be around -100 degrees Fahrenheit (-73 degrees Celsius). This is still warm compared to space, as heat in Earth's core would create some warmth. Humans would probably die from cold and hunger in weeks after the Sun's disappearance. Earth could collide with another drifting planet, too. Don't worry though, in five billion years' time maybe we'll have found another planet to live on!

HANDS-ON SCIENCE

Try the Lunchbox Challenge

You will need: Your lunchbox

Have you ever thought about where all your food comes from? Look at your lunchbox and try and work out if the food in it could exist without the Sun. Does the food come from a plant? Does the food come from an animal? What does that animal eat? Could the animal survive if there were no plants? Is there any food that could be produced without any sunshine?

Galaxy Quiz

Are you a galaxy genius? Test your skills with this quiz and see if you know your white dwarfs from your red giants!

1. Which of these statements is correct?
   a) Earth travels around the Sun
   b) The Sun travels around Earth

2. What is an orbit?

3. How long does it take for the light from the Sun to reach Earth?
   a) Eight and a half seconds
   b) Eight and a half minutes
   c) Eight and a half hours

4. Does the Earth spin clockwise or counterclockwise?

5. What is a solar eclipse?
   a) When the Sun blocks light from the Moon
   b) When Earth blocks light from the Moon
   c) When the Moon blocks light from the Sun

6. How many moons are there in our solar system?
   a) One
   b) Less than ten
   c) More than one hundred

7. How does the Moon glow?
   a) It reflects light from the Sun
   b) It burns hydrogen
   c) It doesn't glow

8. Which planet has the shortest day?
   a) Earth
   b) Venus
   c) Jupiter

9. What is the main gas that the Sun burns?
   a) hydrogen
   b) oxygen
   c) helium

10. What is a red giant?
   a) A large planet
   b) A stage a star goes through when it is dying
   c) A colorful sunset

Glossary

axis (AK-sis) A straight line on which an object turns or seems to turn.

corona (kuh-ROH-nah) A faintly colored luminous ring appearing to surround a star (such as the Sun).

counterclockwise (kown-ter-KLOK-wyz) Moving in the opposite direction that the hands of a clock move.

dwarf planet (DWARF PLA-net) A body that orbits the sun and has a spherical shape but is not large enough to disturb other objects from its orbit.

dwarf star (DWARF STAR) Any star of average or low luminosity, mass, and size.

earthshine (URTH-shyn) Where the Moon's dark area is slightly lit by sunlight reflecting from Earth's surface.

eclipse (ih-KLIPS) A darkening of the Sun or Moon when light from the Sun is blocked by the Moon or the Moon passes through the Earth's shadow.

equator (ih-KWAY-tur) The imaginary line around Earth that separates it into two parts, northern and southern.

gravity (GRA-vih-tee) The force that causes objects to move toward each other. The more material an object is made of, the more gravity it has.

hydrogen (HY-dreh-jen) A colorless gas that weighs less than any other known kind of matter.

light-years (LYT–yeers) The distance traveled by a beam of light in one year.

lunar phases (LOO-ner FAYZ-ez) The different shapes of the Moon as seen from Earth.

mass (MAS) The amount of matter in something.

nuclear fusion (NOO-klee-ur FYOO-zhun) The result of atoms' nuclei combining and releasing energy.

orbit (OR-bit) A circular path around another object or point.

photosphere (FOH-toh-sfeer) The surface of the Sun.

planetary nebula (PLA-neh-teh-ree NEH-byoo-luh) A lit-up, round cloud of dust and gas that forms as an old star dies.

red giant (RED JY-int) A very large star of high luminosity and low surface temperature.

solar system (SOH-ler SIS-tem) The group of planets and other bodies that circle the Sun.

white dwarf (WYT DWARF) A small very dense star that is typically the size of a planet, formed when a low-mass star has exhausted all its central nuclear fuel and lost its outer layers.

Further Information

Books

Gribbin, Mary. *Stars* (Know About). London, UK: National Maritime Museum, 2010.

Lawrence, Ellen. *The Sun* (Zoom into Space). New York, NY: Bearport, 2014.

Due to the changing nature of Internet links, PowerKids Press has developed an online list of websites related to the subject of this book. This site is updated regularly. Please use this link to access the list:
www.powerkidslinks.com/tgg/nightday

Index

A
annular eclipse 11
asteroids 5

C
corona 7, 10
craters 12

D
dwarf planets 23
dwarf star 21

E
earthshine 15

G
Galilei, Galileo 21
Ganymede 21
gravity 5, 17, 26

H
hydrogen 6, 18, 19

L
light pollution 16
light-years 17
lunar phases 13, 14, 15

M
Moon, the 4, 10, 11, 12, 13, 14, 15
moons, other 20, 21

N
nuclear fusion 17

O
orbits 5, 12, 21, 22, 23
Orion's belt 17

P
photosphere 7
planetary nebula 19
planets, other 22, 23

R
red giants 19
rotation of Earth 8, 9

S
Sirius 17
solar eclipse 10, 11
solar system 4, 5, 22
stars 4, 16, 17, 21
Sun, the 4, 5, 6, 7, 8, 9, 10, 11, 13, 14, 15, 16, 18, 19, 21, 24, 25, 26, 27

W
white dwarf 19

Answers
1. a)
2. a journey around an object in space
3. b)
4. counterclockwise
5. c)
6. c)
7. a)
8. c)
9. a)
10. b)